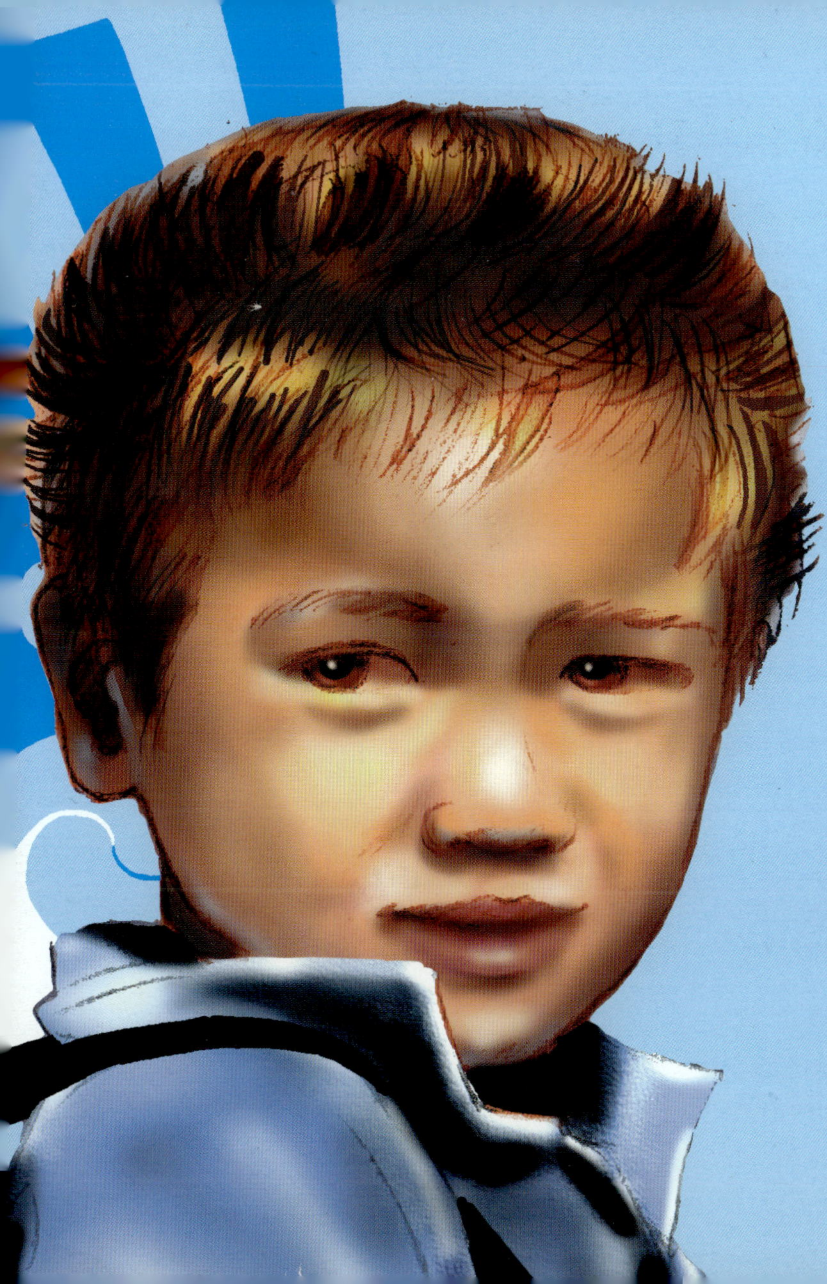

Ngātai Remembers

by Noel Epapara
as told to Barbara Moore

illustrations by
Vaitoa Baker

Learning Media
Wellington

When Ngātai was little,
his family lived in Rotorua,
but then they moved to Auckland.

Ngātai remembers the mountains.

He remembers the lake.

He remembers the geysers
and the steam.

Ngātai even remembers
the smell of the sulphur.
He kind of liked that smell.

But, most of all,
he remembers his whānau.

He remembers his koro
walking with him to kōhanga reo.

He remembers his cousin Mahue
pulling him in a trolley.

He also remembers their meeting house
and all the people there.

Rotorua was a good place to live.

But now Ngātai likes Auckland too!
Roka is his new friend at kōhanga reo.
They make kites together.

Whaea Māka helps them
to make books.
Ngātai and Roka tell the story
and make the pictures.
Whaea Māka writes down their words.
Tumeke!

When Koro rings up every Saturday,
Ngātai and Koro kōrero Māori on the phone.
Ngātai reads the books he makes at kōhanga reo,
and Koro says, “Ka pai, e Moko!”

Ngātai still misses Rotorua, though.
He especially misses Koro.

"Don't worry," says Mum.
"We all miss Rotorua
and everybody down there."

Then Mum says, "I'll tell you what.
Dad and I've been thinking."

"What?" says Ngātai.
"What have you been thinking?"

"Well, why don't we go down to Koro's
at Christmas? What about that idea?"

"Cool!" says Ngātai.
"I'd really like that."

And guess what Koro
gives Ngātai at Christmas.
A camera!

Koro helps Ngātai take pictures
of everything around Rotorua
so that he can put them
in a new book at kōhanga reo
to share with Roka.